Sometimes, only one person is missing,

and the whole world seems depopulated.

- Alphonse De Lamartine

GRIEF ENCOUNTERS · VOLUME ONE
TWO PLAYS BY BAMBI EVERSON

Finding Andrew
Dad's Home

GRIEF ENCOUNTERS · VOLUME ONE
TWO PLAYS BY BAMBI EVERSON

Finding Andrew
Dad's Home

**EVERSON
COLEMAN**

NEW YORK

AUTHOR'S NOTE

People often ask me where my bizarre ideas come from, to which I always respond, "Do you know me?" I was brought up loving the macabre. Horror and ghosts were a staple in the Everson lexicon. "Dad's Home" was originally a 20-minute short play written in 2018, when it seemed like every day there was another piece of inconceivable bad news bombarding us. Shane Fleming, Jill Shely, Josh Liveright, and Matt Corry performed it most deftly at my writers group, where I was encouraged to expand it.

Then COVID hit, so on a shelf in my brain it stayed. I was paralyzed with despair and grief as my world shut down. I watched my friends, family, and co-workers get sick or flee NYC. I could not write. What got me through the next 18 months was mentoring young playwrights at PPAS (Professional Performing Arts School). Through little Zoom boxes, these middle-schoolers were creating art, showing up, supporting each other, and managing to have a positive outlook during these dark times.

When I met 12-year-old Leo Kettells, "Dad's Home" was catapulted to the forefront of my mind, and I continued the play with him in mind. It had a Zoom read in the spring of 2021 with Leo Kettells, Travis Schweiger, Tammy McNeill and Matt Corry. I am grateful to them all. "Finding Andrew" came from a Facebook comment from my friend, Virginia Urban, who enjoyed spooky graveyard tours, and another friend who posted a photo of a grave of a child.

I already knew I wanted to work with my PPAS students. I wrote "Finding Andrew" alongside my talented young playwrights. In the spring of 2021, it was part of K/Q's Collective's Short Play festival, on Zoom. Special thanks to Carlie Priso for participating in that, and being a pivotal part of the development.

Ava Wanko joined the "Finding Andrew" team for the EAT production. Having been in a prior reading, I knew her dedication matched her talent and it was a delight to work with her again.

Having school in a tiny Zoom box certainly had its challenges. I was eager to see this play with a live audience. When Paul Adams asked me to participate in the Fall New Works Series at Emerging Artists Theatre in 2021, I was honored and grateful to bring these actors aboard.

I am also indebted to Lynda Crawford and the friends and members of K/Q Collective, who supported the development of the piece.

I am grateful to Matt Corry and Anthony Goss, who have been in a number of my plays and always bring fresh ideas with them, and Michelle Kuchuk, who has given life and encouragement to my work. To my darling Frank Coleman, I owe you everything because without you, none of this could have happened. You opened up my world. And my angel director, Job Christenson, who sees things in my work I never saw myself.

Lastly, I need to thank all of you who have supported me through both the dark and lighter periods of my life. There is no theater without an audience. You are a vital part of this adventure, and my heart's gratitude knows no bounds.

I hope you enjoy reading these plays as much as I loved working on them.

Thank you.

Bambi Everson
New York City, August 2021

FINDING ANDREW - PRODUCTION HISTORY

Zoom reading - K/Q Short Play Festival, NYC - 2021
With Carlie Priso, Leo Kettells, and Bambi Everson.

Staged reading – Emerging Artists Theater, NYC – 2021
With Ava Wanko, Leo Kettells, and Bambi Everson.

Leo Kettells and Ava Wanko (l to r)

DAD'S HOME – PRODUCTION HISTORY

Workshop – K/Q Collective, NYC - 2018
With Shane Fleming, Jill Shely, Josh Liveright, and Matt Corry.

Zoom reading - K/Q Collective, NYC – 2021
With Leo Kettells, Travis Schweiger, Tammy McNeill, and Matt Corry.

Staged reading – Emerging Artists Theater, NYC – 2021
With Leo Kettells, Matt Corry, Michelle Kuchuk, and Anthony Goss.

Anthony Goss, Leo Kettells, Michelle Kuchuk, and Matt Corry (l to r).

Finding Andrew

Bambi Everson

FINDING ANDREW
By Bambi Everson

One act, approximately 22 minutes

CHARACTERS

VIRGINIA (12) – Pragmatic, honest, carrying a heavy burden.
MAX (12) – Virginia's best friend. Wisecracking, protective.
CATHERINE MARSHALL (40s-50s) – Friend of Max's family.
Struggling with severe loss.

PLACE: Brooklyn, NY.
TIME: The present.

SYNOPSIS

Twelve-year-old Virginia's peculiar connection to Andrew is met with
uncertainty and doubt by her best friend, Max.

SCENE 1

VIRGINIA and MAX are walking together, just enjoying each other's company, and taking in the sights.

VIRGINIA
I used to live here.

MAX
Brooklyn?

VIRGINIA
No. Here.

MAX
This is a graveyard.

VIRGINIA
I know.

MAX
It's been a graveyard for... I don't know... a hundred years, maybe.

VIRGINIA
I know!

MAX
You are creeping me out. When did you go goth?

VIRGINIA
Never. I just like black.

MAX
Then what are you talking about?

VIRGINIA
You're going to think I'm weird.

MAX
I already do. But, "good weird."

VIRGINIA
I wanted to tell you for a while, but I wasn't sure myself. Something keeps drawing me back here. Sometimes, when I get close, I get a pain in my chest. Like I am heartsick. But other times, I just sit and... I don't know... have a silent chat. It's over here.

VIRGINIA shows MAX a particular grave.

MAX
Andrew Marshall? Not even funny, Virginia. His mom is one of my mom's best friends. Come on, let's go.

VIRGINIA
He was 11, right?

MAX
You can see that right here. 1998-2009.

VIRGINIA
I was born in 2009.

MAX
So was I. So were a billion other kids. What are you getting at?

VIRGINIA
I know him.

MAX
You couldn't possibly.

VIRGINIA
But I do. Brown hair. Green eyes. Everyone loved his eyelashes. His room had a giant Ramones poster. His mom hated it. I love the Ramones!

MAX

Everyone loves The Ramones. They're awesome.

VIRGINIA

So, here's the thing. I never really felt connected to my mom. That mother/daughter bond... We don't even look alike, really. I always felt like an outsider. Like I was adopted or something, but I wasn't. I know I came out of her body because my dad took a video of my birth. Well, most of it anyway. It went black at a certain point.

MAX

So you think something happened? An alien abduction?

VIRGINIA

No. My dad just fainted is all.

MAX

Did you ever think you were one of those kids switched at birth? I mean, it used to happen every so often in the old days. I think hospitals are more careful now, but you never know. Did you ever think about investigating that? That would make a heck of a lot more sense than... this!

VIRGINIA

I couldn't. My mom is uber-sensitive. I think that would really hurt her feelings. That's not it, anyway. I know I'm connected to Andrew in some profound way that I don't fully understand. I am accessing his feelings and thoughts. They are flowing through me... pumping my heart. I know he wants... I want... to let his family know. Do you think it would give Andrew's parents some comfort to know some part of him is still here?

MAX

I don't know. How am I supposed to know? You're telling me - what? That you are some kind of reincarnated soul?

VIRGINIA

I don't know what or who I am.

MAX

The Marshalls are good people. I don't know their views on the afterlife or reincarnation. It doesn't exactly come up in dinner conversations, but this kind of stuff would certainly mess with someone's mind, don't ya think? It's certainly messing with mine. My mom told me she was pregnant with me when Andrew died. They still came to her baby shower. Can you imagine?

VIRGINIA

He was shot, right?

MAX

Yeah. By a stray bullet. He was just going to the Bodega for bread and milk. His mom sent him out. All this time and you can still see the sadness in her eyes. I don't think she's ever forgiven herself.

VIRGINIA

He didn't feel anything. It was instant. He didn't even know what hit him.

MAX

How do you know?

VIRGINIA

I told you. I just know. I need to meet them. If a part of me is their son, then they might be my parents.

MAX

You know this sounds completely nutso, right?

VIRGINIA

Why do you think I've never ever talked about it before? I felt crazy for years. Afraid I'd be put in a psych ward if I told anyone. You are my best friend. If I can't trust you, who can I trust?

MAX

I think I should talk to my mom about this.

VIRGINIA

No. Your mom will talk to my mom.

MAX

Not if I...

VIRGINIA

Not for nothing, Max, you know I love your mom, but she can't keep a secret. Remember your "surprise" party?

MAX

Ha-ha. Right. That was some good acting, though, on my part.

VIRGINIA

Award winning. Remember when Kate's dad had a thing with our music teacher? News spread quicker than a firecracker fuse, once your mom got wind of it.

MAX

Ok, ok. My mom is a blabbermouth. How do you remember this stuff?

VIRGINIA

My brain is an overflowing file cabinet. Problem is... not all the files are mine. I thought about going by their house, but that felt kinda stalker-y and weird.

MAX

It's pretty darn weird any way you slice it.

VIRGINIA

Will you take me?

MAX
Jeez, Virginia, You 're really putting me in an awkward position.

VIRGINIA
Just introduce me. Let me see if I feel anything at all. Maybe this is all in my head.

MAX
And then what?

VIRGINIA
Then... Nothing. If I feel nothing, if they feel nothing... I clearly need professional help. Please, Max? Just a quick hello. I can't keep this inside anymore.

MAX
I think this is a mistake. You are really serious, right?

VIRGINIA
Dead serious.

MAX
OK, fine. Just let me do all the talking, OK?

VIRGINIA
Thank you. Thank you so much.

MAX
Anything to get out of this graveyard.

END OF SCENE

SCENE 2

VIRGINIA and MAX are walking towards the house.

VIRGINIA
Stop. This is their house. Why are you walking past it?

MAX
Testing your spidey sense. OK. Now what? Do you really need to do this?

VIRGINIA looks up at the windows.

VIRGINIA
That was my room. It used to have a black shade. Paper, from IKEA, I think. That seashell is from a trip to Catalina when I was nine.

MAX
File that under Stop It!! I can't believe you talked me into this. Here goes nothing. Remember, I do the talking.

MAX knocks tentatively.

MAX
They're probably not even home.

VIRGINIA
A dog couldn't hear that knock. Ring the doorbell.

MAX
I think we'd better...

VIRGINIA
Jesus, Max!

VIRGINIA leans in front of MAX and presses the doorbell.

MAX
I changed my mind. Let's go.

MAX takes VIRGINIA's hand and starts to pull her away. The door opens. CATHERINE MARSHALL enters.

CATHERINE
Max?

MAX
Hi, Mrs. Marshall.

CATHERINE
So good to see you. Your mother ok?

MAX
Much better. Thanks for asking.

CATHERINE
Let me think... Last time I saw you was... the 5th grade talent show. Come in, come in. I rarely get visitors these days. Do you still play the guitar?

MAX
Yeah, I do.

VIRGINIA
He had a performance last week. He's so good.

CATHERINE
You should have told me.

MAX
Just a school thing, no big deal.

CATHERINE
So what are you selling today? Come in out of the heat, let me get my purse.

CATHERINE beckons. VIRGINIA and MAX look at each other. They step inside the house. VIRGINIA is looking around.

CATHERINE
Make yourselves comfortable. Max, you got so tall. Can I offer you two a drink or something?

MAX
No. Actually, we're not selling anything. I wanted you to meet my friend Virginia.

CATHERINE
She's lovely. Is she your girlfriend?

MAX
Ewwww. No. Just a friend friend.

VIRGINIA
God! Am I that bad?

MAX
I didn't mean it like that. I just...

CATHERINE
It's OK, Honey. Give him a couple years. Boys mature much slower than girls. So, Ginny...

VIRGINIA
Vir-Ginia. Sorry. I always hated nicknames.

CATHERINE
My boy did, too. He was always Andrew. Even at 2. Never Andy.

VIRGINIA
I know. When "Toy Story" was so popular, everyone was calling him Andy. Drove him nuts.

CATHERINE
(not picking up the clue)
I forgot that. The original was a little before your time, no?

MAX
(giving VIRGINIA a dirty look)
Virginia's a Disney freak. A walking encyclopedia.

VIRGINIA
(to MAX, quietly)
I'm sorry.

MAX
Actually, maybe I would like something to drink, Mrs. Marshall, if it's not too much trouble.

CATHERINE
Of course. Some ice tea? A Coke?

MAX
Either is fine. Thank you.

CATHERINE
And you, Virginia?

VIRGINIA
I'm good, thanks.

CATHERINE exits.

MAX
What was that?

VIRGINIA
I am sorry. It just slipped out. I don't even think she caught on.

MAX
Yeah we may have dodged a bullet... no pun intended. But from now on...

VIRGINIA
Max, this is for real. I know this house. The kitchen has an avocado green fridge. There is a picture of Andrew from little league in a frame. I... I mean, Andrew, gave it to her on Mother's Day when he was eight. My room, upstairs, is still my room. She hasn't changed a thing. She even washed all the dirty clothes under the bed.

CATHERINE enters with a cold glass of ice tea.

CATHERINE
I made it myself. Raspberry Hibiscus. I have honey if...

MAX
No, this is great. Thanks.

MAX gulps it down nervously.

CATHERINE
Come to think of it, Max, I still have a lot of Andrew's things upstairs. Don't know why it's coming to mind right now. Might be a bit outdated, but...

VIRGINIA
Vintage is always cool. Max doesn't like the Yankees, or football, or any sports, really. But I do. I always had a thing for the Tampa Bay Buccaneers. I know we are not supposed to romanticize cutthroat pirates, but football itself is pretty ruthless in and of itself, don't you think?

CATHERINE
I do. Well, honey, I could bag up some stuff for you. I'd been thinking it was past time...

VIRGINIA
That would be AMAZ–

MAX
Actually, Virginia has something she wants to talk to you about.

VIRGINIA
I thought you said...

MAX
You've already revealed your super powers. I'm sorry, Mrs. Marshall. We probably should have written a letter or something. This is so awkward.

CATHERINE
You have something to tell me? What is it honey?

VIRGINIA
My name is Virginia Leonard.

CATHERINE
Do I know your parents?

VIRGINIA
I don't think so. They're not exactly the social type. I was born on March 23rd 2009, at 5:35 pm.

CATHERINE
I see.

VIRGINIA
I see, too.

MAX
Crazy coincidence, right?

CATHERINE
Are you sure it was 5:35?

VIRGINIA
That's what it says on my birth certificate. Here's the thing. I almost died. I had to have immediate heart surgery. A hole in my heart.

CATHERINE
(in shock)
That must have been awful for your parents.

VIRGINIA
Mom says that was the worst and best day of her life. The doctor said without surgery, I wouldn't live 6 months. I'm fine now. I don't remember any of it. What I do remember is being shot, right here. I have this birthmark.

VIRGINIA lifts up her shirt to show a birthmark over her third rib. CATHERINE gasps.

CATHERINE
My son... He was...

VIRGINIA
I know. Was he an organ donor?

CATHERINE
No. By the time the police identified him, it was too late. The police kept the bullet for evidence.

VIRGINIA
This is going to be weird..

MAX
Like it's not weird already?

VIRGINIA
I can feel Andrew.

CATHERINE
Feel him how? Max? What is this?

MAX
Honestly, Mrs. Marshall, I don't know. I've known Virginia since 3rd grade. She doesn't make stuff up. I mean she watches a lot of movies...

VIRGINIA
Max!

MAX
Even so, she's always been an honest person. I never told her anything about Andrew, and yet somehow she knew. She knew things I didn't even know. It's freaking me out big time, so if you want us to leave... Just please don't tell my mom.

CATHERINE
Look at me, Virginia. If this is a prank, just stop it now. If you read about this in the papers or....

VIRGINIA
No. I would never do anything to hurt another person. I'm a Girl Scout. I volunteer at the food bank.

MAX
That's true. Every Sunday. I go, too.... well, once...

CATHERINE
Virginia, how can you feel my son?

VIRGINIA

I always felt there was a part of me that belonged to someone else. I didn't know it was Andrew. I was lured... pulled like a magnet to his grave. I'd never been there before. I've never even been to a graveyard, except for my grandpa, and that was in Florida. I'd go there and hear... not really hear, feel a voice in my head. Me, but not me. Shared knowledge. I know he felt no pain when he was hit.

CATHERINE

The police told me it was instantaneous, but I never believed it. People tell you anything to relieve the suffering of the survivors.

VIRGINIA

It's true. The bodega man... his name is Louie... screamed for him to drop. He rushed over to him after the shot and tried CPR, but it was too late. The bullet went through his rib, up through his heart and out his back. Louie has never gotten over it. He thinks the bullet was meant for him, but no one ever tried again. Louie's an honest guy, didn't owe money... didn't have problems with anyone, but he still blames himself every day. Sometimes he sees you go past the Bodega. He wants to run out to you, but he's so afraid. Even now. So many years later. Louie's retiring soon. Going back to Columbia. He wants to hug you. He is so sorry. Is this too much all at once? I can leave.

CATHERINE

No. Please... May I hug you?

VIRGINIA

I wish you would.

They hug.

CATHERINE

That's nice. Andrew gave great hugs. Some kids decide they are too old for hugs from their mom. Andrew never did. I have missed those hugs so much.

27

VIRGINIA

He's here, somehow. I'm him, or he's me. We're... one. When I hugged
you, I felt closer to you than my own mom. I knew... I knew I would.

MAX

Wow. This is intense. Are you OK, Mrs. Marshall?

CATHERINE

I'm shaking. Look at my hands.

She holds out shaking hands. VIRGINIA takes them and holds them.

CATHERINE

So warm. His hands were always so warm. Thanks for bringing her,
Max. I know that had to be a tough decision to make.

MAX

I'm so confused. Virginia's my best friend, and if she's... and you and
my mom are so close, then...

CATHERINE

We're all connected.

MAX

That sounds like a TV show I watch! What do we do with this? Where
do we go from here?

CATHERINE

My ex-husband would never believe me. Our marriage couldn't sustain
the loss. He has a new family now.

MAX

I know. Mom won't speak to him. If she sees him in the grocery store,
she turns and heads up another aisle putting random things in her cart
and forgetting to take them out. We have every species of Oreo known to
mankind.

CATHERINE
As if a new person could supplant...

VIRGINIA
He didn't forget. How could he? Andrew was his spitting image. He just
felt it was healthier for him to move forward. He has tons of pictures in a
shoebox in the closet. It hurts too much to have them on display, to have
to answer questions whenever a visitor asks if that is him as a little boy.
His wife... She's not a bad person. She's focusing on their daughter, but
she's never negated the importance Andrew in his dad's life. I'm sorry
you all don't talk.

CATHERINE
Sometimes grief unites a family. Not in this case. I couldn't move
forward when everything I loved was behind me. Friends suggested I get
a dog, an outlet for all the love I've bottled up. They don't understand. I
don't want another living thing in this house. Our little backyard pond
used to have goldfish. I can't keep up. I can't garden. Everything is dead
or dying and I shouldn't be responsible ever for another living thing. It's
my fault Andrew's gone, and all I want is forgiveness, but there is no one
to forgive me.

VIRGINIA
Take my hands.

CATHERINE does.

VIRGINIA (cont.)
I need you to hear this.
(closes her eyes and concentrates)
You do not need to be forgiven. When I came home from school that
day, I ate two peanut butter and jelly sandwiches, and drank all the milk.
Chocolate milk, of course. I didn't tell you because I knew I'd still be
hungry for dinner in an hour. It's my fault, not yours, that I had to go to
the Bodega. You always gave me everything I needed, and you protected
me the best you could. I love you Mama. I'm still here.

VIRGINIA opens her eyes. CATHERINE is clearly different. She is crying, but seems happy.

VIRGINIA
Mrs. Marshall? I'm not sure what just happened.

MAX
Everybody OK here? 'Cause I for one am a little freaked out.

CATHERINE
I'm good. Not to get all ET about it, but I feel him. Right here. I have always thought something remains after death. Memories. My darling Virginia, I think you were a sender. My wingless angel. How do you feel?

VIRGINIA
Frankly, a little empty, but in a good way. I'm going to miss him.

MAX
You still like the Ramones, though?

VIRGINIA
Everyone likes the Ramones. They're awesome!

MAX
That's a relief. I was worried I would lose my best friend.

VIRGINIA
Nope. Still here. Your favorite weirdo.

CATHERINE
Thank you for bringing Andrew home.

MAX
My mom always said life is stronger than death. She says a lot of things, but I never paid attention to what old people say... No offense, Mrs. Marshall.

CATHERINE
Thank you for uniting my grief. It always had two lives. The lie where I pretend I am alright, and the one that has my heart crying out in agony. My pain was this big hole, and I kept falling in it and trying to claw my way out, only to see I was digging myself deeper. I think now I can see the hole and try to walk around it. I'll never be the same again. I don't want to be. There is a place in me, the keeper of Andrew's memories, that death will never touch.

MAX
Well, I guess we should be going now. This has certainly been an interesting day.

CATHERINE
You'll come back, won't you, Virginia? Anytime. The clothes...

VIRGINIA
Sure.

CATHERINE
You too, Max. Don't be a stranger.

MAX
I couldn't be. Not after this.

VIRGINIA hugs CATHERINE again. Deeply and long.

VIRGINIA
Yup. He's gone. He's all yours, Mrs. Marshall.

MAX
What now?

CATHERINE
I'm going to go to that Bodega. Hug that man...?

VIRGINIA
I don't remember...

MAX
His name is Louie.

CATHERINE
Yes. Louie. I remember now. And you, Virginia?

VIRGINIA
I am going home to hug my mom. I think she's been waiting a long time.

BLACKOUT

END OF PLAY

Dad's Home

Bambi Everson

DAD'S HOME
One act, approx. 50 minutes.

CHARACTERS
PAUL KETRO - Dad
JEREMY KETRO - Son
MICHELLE KETRO-CRAWFORD - Mom
JOHN CRAWFORD - Michelle's husband

TIME: The present.
PLACE: The family's apartment.

SYNOPSIS: Paul is home from the office. Something is terribly wrong, and everybody knows but him.

SCENE 1

PAUL enters the apartment with his key. He hangs up his coat.

PAUL
Hi honey, I'm home!

JEREMY, PAUL's teenage son enters.

JEREMY
Dad!

PAUL
Hey pal, how was your day?

JEREMY
Fine... Great!

JEREMY gives his dad a hug, maybe a fist bump and goes towards the bedroom.

JEREMY (Cont.)
Stay right there. Um... Mom... Dad's home.

MICHELLE
(offstage)
Awww... Sweetie. That's the first time I heard you call him dad.

JEREMY
No. Mom... I mean Dad's HOME. As in, Dad!

PAUL
And man oh man... am I exhausted! Tough day at the office. Any plans for dinner? I am fine with ordering in. What's up with Mom?

JEREMY
She's changing. We have parent teacher conferences tonight.

PAUL

Oh. That's tonight? You're doing fine in school, right? No issues? Not failing anything?

JEREMY

I'm fine. 86 average. Mom! Can you come out please? NOW?

PAUL

That's good, then. No need for me to sit around schmoozing with the other parents. Rene's dad always wants me to go fishing with him. I hate fishing. That guy is so pretentious. Thinks he's better than me because he has a boat. I could have gotten a boat if I wanted one. I chose to invest in our future.

JEREMY

I know. It's all good. Can I get you a beer or something?

PAUL

Since when do we have beer in the house? You don't drink it, right?

JEREMY

I'm 12!

PAUL

(absentmindedly)

When did that happen? Good. No drinking. Just checking. Sure. Thanks, son.

JEREMY runs and gets PAUL a beer.

JEREMY

Here ya go. I'll, um... be right back.

JEREMY runs off stage. We hear him talking to his mother. PAUL makes himself totally at home. Takes off his shoes, Drinks his beer. Looks around. A few things are different. He might move a chair or an object to a different spot.

JEREMY
Mom. You gotta come out NOW. I am telling you Dad's here. On the couch. Like nothing happened.

MICHELLE
That's not even funny.

JEREMY
Do you see me laughing? I am serious. Dead serious. See for yourself.

MICHELLE and JEREMY peek out from the bedroom and see PAUL.

MICHELLE
OH MY GOD!!

JEREMY
Told you. I am not hallucinating.

MICHELLE
What do we do?

JEREMY
How am I supposed to know? It's not like I have any experience with this sort of thing.

PAUL
Michelle? What's up?

MICHELLE enters tentatively with JEREMY behind her. PAUL approaches. MICHELLE screams!

PAUL
What's up?

JEREMY
BUG! Big Bug.
(stomps his foot)
Got it!!

PAUL
Hi, honey. Looking good.

He goes to kiss her. She backs up a little.

PAUL
Do I smell?
(checks himself)

MICHELLE
No, sorry. Makeup.

MICHELLE kisses him gently on the cheek.

MICHELLE
How are you feeling?

PAUL
To be honest, pretty dead. I think I am going to crash for a few. What time are you leaving?

MICHELLE
I think I'm changing my mind. I don't think I am going to go anywhere tonight.

JEREMY
Good call, Mom.

PAUL
Awesome. Let's order Chinese. Wake me when it comes.

PAUL exits into the bedroom.

MICHELLE
What is going on?

JEREMY
He doesn't know. But it's going to be mighty sticky when John gets home.

MICHELLE
Oh God!! John. He's flying back today. I'll call.

JEREMY
You can't call. John gave me his cell while he was away.

MICHELLE
Why?

JEREMY
Because he's the soccer coach, Mom. I'm fielding calls. I told you I needed a cell phone.

MICHELLE
You're too young.

JEREMY
I'm 12! And FYI, mom, I am the only kid in the school without a cell phone.

MICHELLE
I'll email him.

JEREMY
Sure, mom. Like he's going to check emails on the way home. He's like the Eveready Bunny… Bounding through customs, just to get home five minutes earlier.

MICHELLE
What do I do? I know - go downstairs and put a note on the door.

JEREMY
Saying what?

PAUL
(offstage)
Hard to nap with you two conspiring. It's Chinese food, not a Russian conspiracy. Do you need a mediator?

MICHELLE AND JEREMY
No / Haha / We got this Dad. Rest up.

JEREMY hands MICHELLE the phone. She hands it back. There is some silent conversation. Finally, MICHELLE grabs the phone and dials.

MICHELLE
Hello? Yes. Delivery. That's right. Me again. Michelle. Apartment 8A. One General Tso's chicken. What does dad like, again?

JEREMY
Beef with snow peas. At least when he...

MICHELLE
Right. One beef with snow peas. Two egg rolls. No, three. What do you want, honey?

JEREMY
Chicken wings.

MICHELLE
One order of four chicken wings, and ginger ale? Oh... Three. Ok, great.
Thanks.
(hangs up)
Now what?

JEREMY
Well, he's going to know something's up when he opens the closet, or
uses the bathroom. Mom! The pictures!

MICHELLE quickly takes them down and hides them somewhere
ridiculous. Under the couch or something.

MICHELLE
It's been a year. I mean, what did he expect?

JEREMY
Mom, I don't think he expected anything. Do we tell him?

MICHELLE
Tell him that he died?? You can't just spring this on someone!
(pause)
Do you think someone put pot in the tuna casserole?

JEREMY
I didn't eat that. I hate Tuna Mac. Mom, he is here. We both saw him.
And not like in one of those zombie movies, when they come back with
bullet holes in their heads. He looks fine. He looks like Dad. He *is* Dad.

MICHELLE
Your dad is gone. I saw the body.

JEREMY
Are you sure? Maybe they made some kind of mistake. Maybe it just
looked like dad. After all, they all wear the same god-awful powder blue
shirts and khaki pants. Maybe he gave his wallet to someone else that
day. Maybe dad's had amnesia. This stuff happens all the time.

MICHELLE
In the movies. It happens on TV. Not in real life. I think I would
recognize your father, even with half his head gone.

JEREMY
So, how do you explain this?

MICHELLE
I can't. Go online. See if anyone has posted any paranormal
phenomenon.

JEREMY
The Internet is full of nuts, mom. A thousand people post how their cat is
really their dead grandmother.

MICHELLE
Look anyway. Maybe someone from the office. Check in on Shalisa. She
lost her husband, too.

JEREMY
She's YOUR friend. YOU ask her if her dead husband suddenly came
waltzing into the house, wanting dinner.

MICHELLE
Just go look at her Facebook page. Check the Memorial page for
Henderson, Bryce and Coleman. See if anyone posted anything.

JEREMY
What are you going to do?

MICHELLE
I am going to set the table for dinner.

*JEREMY goes to his laptop and starts checking around. PAUL comes
staggering out of the bedroom wearing a shirt that does not quite fit.*

PAUL
Honey?

JEREMY slams down the computer.

MICHELLE
Food's not here yet, sweetie. Why don't you just go lie down?

PAUL
I don't remember this shirt. Did the laundry screw up again?

MICHELLE
No, we are having a... clothing drive for the homeless.

JEREMY looks at his mom strangely.

MICHELLE
I, uh... volunteered to hold all the men's clothes in the closet. Sorry. I'll take them out.

PAUL
No, no... That's fine. Nice clothes. Any in my size?

MICHELLE
No!

JEREMY
Dad, the whole point is, to help the homeless look really good when they go for job interviews. Right, Mom? I mean, you already look good, Dad, and you have a job, right? You remember your job, don't you?

PAUL.
Not likely to forget a place I've worked at for 12 years! You remember *your* job, son? Homework done?

JEREMY
They don't give us homework on parent/teacher conference day.

PAUL
You look taller.

JEREMY
Yeah, well, I've been working out.

PAUL
Since this morning.

MICHELLE
Feels like every day, he grows another inch. Had to buy all new pants last month.

Buzzer sounds.

MICHELLE
Food's here!

PAUL
I'll get it.
(reaches for his wallet)

MICHELLE
No! I got it. Go sit down. Jeremy, get your dad a beer.

JEREMY
I already got him one.

MICHELLE
So... Get him another!

PAUL
Guess I'll just change outta this shirt.

MICHELLE
Nah, It's fine New look for you. I, uh... like that color on you. Sexy.
Makes your eyes pop. I love you.

*MICHELLE has a quick encounter with the unseen delivery guy,
exchanging pleasantries, and puts the food on the table. PAUL starts
attacking it voraciously.*

PAUL
(gulping down food)
Oh, my God! I am famished. Feels like I haven't eaten in months!

JEREMY
Years, I bet. Whoa!! Dad! Easy does it.

PAUL
(stops and begins dishing out the food)
Sorry. Don't know what's gotten into me. Let's all sit. Rice?

JEREMY
Sure.

PAUL
Chicken wings?

JEREMY
Mine. Thanks.

PAUL makes sure everyone has food.

PAUL
This is nice. Us all together. Feels like ages since we've had a family
meal. Life gets so complicated. Nothing is more important than family.

MICHELLE
Honey... Can you tell me how you got here?

PAUL

Next to impossible, I tell you! The A train was running on the F line. No
D. No B. I had to take the C and then the shuttle bus. Honestly, I don't
know how tourists or people who don't speak English get anywhere. I
nearly wound up in Canarsie!

*They eat in silence for a moment. MICHELLE and JEREMY never take
their eyes off PAUL.*

MICHELLE

So.... Tell us about work, dear.

PAUL

You don't want to hear about that.

JEREMY

Yeah, we do. We really do.

MICHELLE

Spare us nothing, dear.

PAUL

(trying to remember)

Well, I was almost late, I made breakfast for Jeremy, but you didn't have
time...

JEREMY

I stop at D 'n' D's before school. All the kids do.

PAUL

Donuts are not breakfast.

MICHELLE

Ok. You got to work...

PAUL

Just barely. Damn trains. And all this work is piled on my desk. Joe was fired...

MICHELLE

I know. He had been stealing from the company for months.

PAUL

How did you know that? We were sworn to secrecy, pending an internal investigation.

MICHELLE

It was all over the... Shalisa told me.

PAUL

That Jeff! Never could keep his mouth shut. I'm going to have a word with him.

JEREMY

Good luck with that one, dad.

PAUL

(slowly piecing his day together)

Anyway, Jackson transferred all Joe's accounts to me. What a mess. I'm looking at an 80-hour week. I go and grab a coffee from the kitchen, and I pass Joe. Guess he was coming to clean out his desk or something. I thought it was weird. He was wearing a trench coat, and it's April. You gonna eat all of those chicken wings, son?

JEREMY

No. Take 'em.

PAUL does and just commences eating. MICHELLE and JEREMY are waiting with anticipation for PAUL to continue.

MICHELLE
(getting up)
Anyone need anything else?

Nobody does.

MICHELLE (Cont.)
Well, I think I need a drink. A real one.

She goes and pours herself a glass of wine and gulps it down quickly.

MICHELLE
You passed Joe in the hallway.

PAUL
(it's coming together now)
Yeah. Then I start working on the Hannagan account. Could not find the
bank conciliations. Some missing documents. Duplicate check numbers.
Musta got lost in crunching numbers for a bit. Then Janis, our secretary
hollered something.

MICHELLE
She hollered?

PAUL
No. She screamed. She screamed GUN! And then... And then I saw Joe.
He pulled something out of his trench coat. A rifle of some sort.

JEREMY
An AR-15. A semi-automatic rifle.

PAUL
(really reliving it now)
I guess. What do I know from guns? There was pandemonium. People
started diving under their desks. I heard a single shot, then another. Max
tried crawling to his girlfriend who was at reception. I saw him go down.
And Fred, and Peter, Cynthia, Kecia, and Charles. Joe was picking us

PAUL (Cont.)

off. One by one. He was looking straight at me. So I said, "Hey Joe, what's going on?" He stopped and stared at me. "Hey," he said to me. And then, "Sorry about this, man. You are one of the good ones." Then he started to walk away. He took a few steps towards Jackson's office, then he turned around and... well, everything went black.

MICHELLE
(hugging him)
OH MY GOD! I am so sorry.

PAUL
I don't remember anything after that. Not until I was coming home. I don't know how I even got out of the building.

MICHELLE
Sweetie... you didn't.

PAUL
What?

MICHELLE
That was over a year ago.

PAUL
No.

JEREMY
The news called you a hero, dad. The survivors said you stood tall and faced him. That you looked so calm, it confused him for a while. Six people got out of that room safely because of you.

PAUL
Survivors?

MICHELLE
There were 30 rounds in that fucking gun. He got through 19 before the police came. Eleven dead. Seven critically injured, Alex escaped with minor injuries, pretending to be dead. Jeff is gone, honey. Max, Stephen, Cody, Melissa, Jackson, Peter, Fred, Charles, and Janis. Dead on the scene. They turned off Julie's life support months ago. There had been no visible brain activity since the incident. They tried to save the baby, but they couldn't.

PAUL
This really happened? I was hoping it was a dream. A nightmare. Poor Julie! We had just thrown her a baby shower.

MICHELLE
It was the biggest office shooting since the Edmond post office in 1986. Fourteen gunned down then. We lost you that day and I have missed you every day since then.

JEREMY
Dad, you're dead.

PAUL
I'm dead? I don't feel dead.

JEREMY
Trust me. You are dead. Like, Abraham Lincoln dead. But it's really good to see you!

MICHELLE
We should go to the hospital or something.

PAUL
Do I still have insurance? From the office?

MICHELLE
Oh, God!! The insurance.

PAUL
What?

MICHELLE
Each family received 300 thousand dollars. Crime victim compensation.
It was supposed to be more, but the city... Well, it's still owed to us.
Honey, I bought our apartment with the money.

PAUL
Cool. That was a good investment. No more rent?

MICHELLE
Maintenance fee. The management gave us a good deal because of... you
know. There was a picture of you in the lobby for months. People
brought flowers. Wrote notes. I still have them. ABC news came and
filmed. Talked to our neighbors. Oh, Lord. Everyone knows what you
look like. They'll think you faked your own death. They'll think we're
frauds. They'll want the insurance money back.

JEREMY
Who cares about the money, Mom? It's a miracle. Grandma always says,
"When a miracle happens, don't stand in its way." We got dad back.
Dead dad is way better than no dad!

MICHELLE
You don't understand. Your dad and I could go to jail. We
misappropriated funds. It's insurance fraud. Unless we can prove he's
really dead!

She grabs his hand and feels for a pulse. Gives JEREMY his other hand.

MICHELLE
Do you feel anything?

JEREMY
I'm not a nurse, mom, but I don't feel anything.

MICHELLE feels his throat. Nothing. Puts her ear to his chest, shakes her head. No heartbeat.

PAUL

Why would he want to hurt us? We were his friends. Joe looked at me and said, "Hey." Like it was a regular Monday. He walked away from me. I was looking at Melissa. The blood was pooling around her face turning her hair black. She gets $400 haircuts. Her eyes were open. I can't forget her eyes... Joe...

MICHELLE

Joe's dead. The police took him down before he reloaded. He had 100 rounds on him. He wasn't finished. No one even knew he had a gun.

PAUL

His wife... his kids...

MICHELLE

They left town. No one has heard from them. The media was vicious. Blamed them. How could they not know what he was planning?

JEREMY

Dad, it really sucked. Like, I used to be friends with Joe Jr. I knew it wasn't his fault but things were just different after. I kept seeing his dad's face in him, and what he did to you. The other kids, too. We didn't know what to do, what to say. We knew we weren't supposed to hate him but we just couldn't help it. Do you think that's why you came back, dad? To fix that? To help his family? All the families?

PAUL

Why me? I don't have any answers. I don't know why he did anything. He never said a word to me.

JEREMY

Can you ask him? Is there a way?

PAUL
I don't know anything about the "other side." All I know is that I had the world's shittiest day at work, and all I wanted to do was come home to my family.

JEREMY
Mom?

MICHELLE shakes her head.

JEREMY
You gotta tell him. Maybe it's part of it.

PAUL
Tell me what, Michelle? This day couldn't possibly get any worse.

MICHELLE
I missed you every single minute of every day. I couldn't work. I couldn't eat. I barely got dressed, forget leaving the house. I didn't want grief counseling. I was grieving just fine. The group were people I only knew from your office parties. Now we were bonded in pain by this horrible thing. I couldn't listen to anyone else's story. I hated the whole world. I was married to my own pain. Every day someone came by with trays of food. They rotted in the fridge. Everyone asked the same ridiculous question, "How am I?" If I told them the truth, that I died with you that day, I got, "You must go on for Jeremy's sake," that "Paul would want you to go on."

PAUL
That's true, though. I would have.

MICHELLE
John was a godsend. He ran interference for me. Made sure Jeremy ate, went to soccer practice, did his homework, let him vent about you. I was so wrapped up in my loss, I didn't have any room to help Jeremy through his.

PAUL
John's always had my back. My brother from another mother. I'm glad
he was there for you. Both of you.

MICHELLE
I don't know what we would have done without him, frankly. Every
battle, every bit of bureaucratic bullshit we had to endure, he was our
crusader. Because he loved you, too. It just seemed natural for us to...
connect... through you. You know... on a deeper level.

PAUL
You slept with my best friend?

MICHELLE
I married him. Four months ago.

PAUL
Fuck.

MICHELLE
It was very small. City Hall. No reception or anything.

JEREMY
Not like your memorial, Dad. The turnout for that was incredible. The
Riverside Chapel was packed. They had to pipe the service onto the
street because no one would leave. The crowd of people went all around
the block. Your old bandmates played "Do You Realize?" Everyone said
you shoulda been there. You would have loved it.

PAUL
Fuck.
(realizing)
So those clothes...

MICHELLE
Yeah. I am so sorry.

PAUL
Where is he?

MICHELLE
Business trip. Paris. He's due back tonight. You're not going to...

PAUL
What? Beat him up? No. Tell him I said thanks.

MICHELLE
What do we do now?

PAUL
I've gotta go lie down. This has been a hell of a day. Ok if I use our bedroom, or would you rather...?

MICHELLE
No. The bedroom. Of course... I never stopped loving you, Paul.

PAUL
Me neither. But I thought I told you that this morning.

JEREMY
Look at the bright side. We have over a year of TV to catch up on. And movies. Lots of bonding time.

JEREMY goes to hug him.

JEREMY
I love you, Dad. Welcome home.

MICHELLE
Yes. Welcome home, dear.

MICHELLE kisses him. PAUL stands stunned for a moment.

PAUL
Good night, son. Love you.

PAUL exits to the bedroom. JEREMY and MICHELLE look at each other as the lights fade. They hear a key rattling in the door. They gasp. JOHN enters.

JOHN
Hi honey, I'm home!

BLACKOUT

SCENE 2

PAUL, MICHELLE, and JOHN are sitting on the couch. JEREMY on a chair to the side. They sit in silence for a while. Finally...

JOHN
Well, this is awkward.

PAUL
Yup.

MICHELLE
Anyone need anything? A drink, maybe?

JEREMY
Yeah, Mom. Dad's back from the dead. It's Miller time! Frankly, I think we all need to be dead sober here. No offense, dad.

PAUL
None taken.
(to JOHN)
I don't hold anything against you, man. I appreciate you taking care of my family while I was... er... gone.

JOHN
Thanks. I loved you like a brother. You know that. Always will.

PAUL
I know.

They hug.

JOHN
You feel just like you. It's nice. Weird as shit, but nice. Should I go? I should go.

MICHELLE
Where? No. How do I...

JEREMY
I've got soccer tomorrow. Big game.

JOHN
I'll be there.

JEREMY
I wish dead dad could come, too.

MICHELLE
No! Why are you talking about soccer? What are you thinking? Paul...
You are legally, actually dead. We collected insurance money. Jeremy's
school had a fundraiser. This isn't exactly an "oops" moment. "Sorry,
he's fine. Just kidding!"

JOHN
Is he fine, though? I mean, you look great, bro, No offense, but maybe he
should see somebody... a doctor. Do we know anyone who makes house
calls? This is an unusual situation.

JEREMY
No.

JEREMY runs to his dad.

MICHELLE
Honey...

JEREMY
No doctor. What if dad is declared dead again and just melts away?
Turns to ash like a vampire? What if the knowing makes him go away
forever? I am not losing him twice. You got to have a new husband,
Mom. I'm not blaming you. John's cool and all that...

JOHN
Thanks.

JEREMY
But if I got to choose... I mean, what kid wouldn't want to have his real
dad back? Ok, maybe Charles Manson's kids...

MICHELLE
I identified your body. Jeremy's eulogy...

JEREMY
I think I have a copy of it on my computer if you wanna...

MICHELLE
And John spoke so beautifully, So much love in that room...

PAUL
Sorry I missed it. I am sure I would have loved it. You know what I
would really love? To not be dead.

JOHN
Of course. We all would have preferred that.

JEREMY
My teacher said the brave never really die. Maybe that's why you are
here.

PAUL
For what purpose? I can't travel through time.

MICHELLE
Maybe there is some piece of information... Something everyone missed.

PAUL
Suddenly, I am flooded with memories. They are coming at me... like the
bullets. I don't want– can't live through that all again. To see the people I
worked with picked off like tin cans in target practice. There must have

PAUL (Cont.)
been signs. I should have seen the signs. I could have supported him.
Helped pay the company back.

JOHN
Dude, you can't blame yourself.

MICHELLE
No one could have predicted such a thing happening. No one did. It's not
your fault.

JEREMY
You are the hero, dad! The hero never dies in the movies. Except for the
Terminator, but he was a robot to begin with.

PAUL
I'm no hero. The heroes win. I didn't win. The monsters won. My friends
are dead, my wife is married.

MICHELLE/ JOHN
Sorry/Really sorry.

PAUL
So, what now? Do we trade nights with Michelle, like a reverse
Mormon?

JOHN
I mean... You are dead. No pulse. Which means no blood. Could you
even...?

JEREMY
Ew!!! Child here, remember? There are some things I still want to be
protected from, thank you!

JOHN
You're right. I'm going to leave. You were here first. You were married
longer.

MICHELLE

I think that's best for now. I'm sorry. But... Paul? What are we going to do? You can't be seen. Did you pass anyone coming home? I mean, we could be in trouble right now.

PAUL

It was night. I don't remember. Obviously, it wasn't strange to me. I was just coming home. I didn't notice.

JEREMY

He can go out at night. There are lots of night games at the stadium. Midnight movies. We can disguise him. Fake mustache, get a beard, dark glasses...

MICHELLE

That is not a solution.

JOHN

Do you know any plastic surgeons? We have money. Well, some...

MICHELLE

Oh, sure. I'll just Google "illicit backstreet plastic surgeons."

JEREMY

Like that movie.

MICHELLE

Dark Passage? When did you see that?

JEREMY

Nah, the one with Nicholas Cage. Face/Off. It's from the 90s. Who would remember? There are all those crazy shows on TV. Guys who get 30 surgeries to look like Justin Bieber.

PAUL

I do NOT want to look like Justin Bieber.

JOHN
We could just wrap up your face like the Invisible Man. I mean, it could
be done. This is New York, after all.

PAUL
And then what? How do I get a job? What do I do for ID? This is a lot
for a person to process.

JEREMY
For us, too, Dad. Every day I see kids with their dads, and I know what
I'm missing. What you were missing. Being the kid of a hero dad, people
expect a lot from me. Like, I am supposed to follow in your footsteps,
doing good, saving kittens from trees, and helping old ladies with their
packages. And when I screw up, they're disappointed, but then they
forgive me, because I'm the kid with a dead dad! I get away with murder.
Oops, sorry. I will never ever be just a regular kid again.

JOHN
I'm gonna go now. I'll stay at the Citizen Downtown. Gonna need my
cell phone, sport.

JEREMY
Oh, yeah.

He goes off stage to get it.

JOHN
(to Michelle)
It's going to be OK.

MICHELLE
How?

JOHN
I always knew I was second best. That you loved him more. I think
maybe I did too.

MICHELLE
(clearly torn)
It's not a matter of loving someone more...
(looks at PAUL and then back again)

PAUL
When I left the house this morning, I was married to the love of my life.

MICHELLE
It's... It's complicated.

JOHN
Just a tad. I'd never betray my best friend.
(to PAUL)
Michelle... and Jeremy... I wanted to do right by them, and you. When it... we... happened, I figured it's what you would have wanted.

JEREMY returns with the cell phone.

JEREMY
Here ya go.

MICHELLE
I'll get you your own tomorrow.

JEREMY
Really?

MICHELLE
It's time.

JOHN
I'll be at the game tomorrow. It'll be good. Talking to the parents. I'll spread some seeds around. Tell them how your mom and I need a little time apart. I will always be here for you sport. All of you. Whatever you need. Hey, let me try something. Stand together.

JOHN takes out his cell phone. The three of them pose for an awkward picture.

JEREMY
Lemme see.
(runs over and looks at the photo)
Mom, look. Clear as day. Dad, you're not a ghost or a vampire.

PAUL
So, what am I?

JOHN
You're home.

JOHN kisses MICHELLE on the cheek.

JOHN
Bye, love. See you tomorrow, sport.

John shakes PAUL's hand and then they hug.

JOHN
Good luck, man. Take care of each other.

JOHN exits. The three stand and stare at each other.

BLACKOUT

SCENE 3

One month later. PAUL is sitting in front of the TV. JEREMY enters from school.

JEREMY
Hey, Dad...

PAUL
How was school, son?

JEREMY
OK, I guess. How's... what are you watching?

PAUL
Sherlock. Never had the time to commit to a series before. Got homework?

JEREMY
Yeah. Duh. Always. Dad, can we not try to have normal conversations every day? Nothing about this is normal.

PAUL
I'm sorry. It must be a horrible burden, holding on to this secret.

JEREMY
Yeah. When you first died, it was awful. I couldn't believe the world was still happening, and I was angry at every day that started without you. My friends helped a lot, but you know what really changed things for me? Girls!

PAUL
Well, of course. You are a good-looking young man. You take after your mother, thank goodness.

JEREMY
I had faced facts, dad. I was short, nerdy and completely invisible to girls. Until you died. Almost overnight, I became this sad, lost puppy that needed to be taken care of. I got homemade chocolate chip cookies. Bread, pies, hugs... I was the only boy invited to the girls' slumber parties.

PAUL
Sounds nice.

JEREMY
It was. But now I can't do any of that stuff. Every day after school, I run home to see you. To make sure you're still here... which you are. But now... YOU are the sad lost puppy, waiting by the door 'til I get home.

PAUL
I didn't realize I was cramping your style. Go. Spend more time with your friends.

JEREMY
And tell them what? That for the last month, I've been walking the streets under the cloak of night with my dead dad? I've always been a crappy liar. I don't know how to talk to people anymore. My teachers worry that I am depressed again, because I have stopped socializing. They notice I'm tired and falling asleep in class.

PAUL
I'm sorry. We will curtail the nighttime wanderings 'til you're back on track.

JEREMY
That's not it, dad. I love our time together. We have so much to catch up on. Things I can't talk about with mom. I need you... Just... No offense, but under normal circumstances, a 12 year old doesn't want to spend all their free time with their parents.
(cont.)

JEREMY (Cont.)
In health class, we are talking about detachment, where we start developing our own opinions, and relying on our peers for help. How can I gain the trust of my friends with a literal and physical specter in my life?

PAUL
Funny you should mention detachment. Today, my foot disappeared.

JEREMY
What? That's random.

PAUL
Yeah, I was just sitting here catching up on TV...I looked down and it was gone. I don't feel any pain, and I can still walk and all, see...
(He demonstrates)
It's a little awkward. I'm wondering if this is the beginning.

JEREMY
Of what?

PAUL
The end, I guess.

JEREMY
No! Can't you do anything?

PAUL
I didn't know I could do this. Heck, maybe it's a fluke. Phantom limbs and such... Oh, crap.

JEREMY
What?

PAUL
There goes the other one. Hmmm. Very peculiar.

JEREMY
I'm calling Mom.

PAUL
Where is Mom?

JEREMY is silent.

PAUL
Never mind. It's Ok.
(pause)
I think he really loves her, huh?

JEREMY
I don't know. Mom's love life is the last thing on my mind.
(pause)
I mean, John's a good guy. A soccer coach. Stuff that's hard... impossible for you. Especially now.

PAUL
I never expected he would walk away from either of you. God knows, I couldn't.

JEREMY
God? You think God brought you here? Sorry, dad. I stopped believing in God when he let a maniac kill my dad, and ten other people.

MICHELLE enters with her key. PAUL and JEREMY stop immediately.

MICHELLE
Sorry I'm a little late... I...

PAUL
It's cool. I understand.

JEREMY
Dad lost his feet.

MICHELLE
(absentmindedly)
Well, they have to be here somewhere, where did you last see them?

JEREMY
At the bottom of his pants! Mom! Dad might be in trouble.

PAUL
I'd say I don't have a leg to stand on, but I seem to be standing just fine.

MICHELLE
What does this mean?

PAUL
Saving money on shoes and socks, for one thing.

JEREMY
Stop with the dad jokes. I think this is your fault, mom.

PAUL/ MICHELLE
That's not fair.

MICHELLE
You think I don't feel guilty enough? I'm stuck between two worlds and I can't... don't want to abandon either one completely.

JEREMY
You don't need Dad the same way anymore, so he's fading away. Well, I still need him.
(to PAUL)
I'm sorry I said that stuff earlier. You are more important than my dumb friends.

PAUL
Even Ginny Taylor?

JEREMY
Yes. Even... Wait– how do you know about her? I never said a word.

PAUL
I have no idea. Gosh... Maybe I am becoming one with the universe, literally.

JEREMY
Evanescent.

MICHELLE
The band? That's a little before your time.

JEREMY
The adjective. Disappearing slowly. Passing out of sight.

PAUL
I think I need a moment with mom.

JEREMY
Fine. But if anything else disappears, you better let me know. I'll be in my room Googling reversing dematerialization.

JEREMY exits.

PAUL
He's a great kid. You did great.

MICHELLE
We did great.
(pause)
I'm sorry.

PAUL
Don't. It's really ok.

MICHELLE

I love you so much.

PAUL

I know.

MICHELLE

Do you remember our housewarming party? Before Jeremy? Gina gave us that basket filled with plants. You made fun of me and my black thumb. You worried what kind of a mother I'd be if I couldn't even keep a plant alive. I worried, too. But I managed. That plant lasted 13 years in that basket, but then after you... it started losing its leaves. Gina said I should have replanted it years ago, that the soil had lost all its nutrients. I was really afraid, but I figured it was the plant's best chance. I was so gentle. But when I lifted it up, I saw the roots were all entangled. Some were waterlogged and broke off in my hand. Still, I gave it a lovely new home in a new pot, Miracle grow soil. I talked to it... and it died within the week. 13 years. I was heartbroken. I never should have tampered. If it was going to die, it should have died a natural death. I traumatized it. I broke the roots and I killed it.

PAUL

Are you speaking in metaphors?

MICHELLE

No. This actually happened. I am a plant murderer. I killed the first living thing we owned collectively.

PAUL

So... what? You think my return is the plant's revenge? I don't know much about death, but I know karma doesn't work like that! Honey, our roots are forever entwined. There is no reason for you to hold on to your guilt. It's a useless emotion. There is a quote, "With loss, there is an even greater presence of love." Our love doesn't go away. It transforms into a different love, a deeper forever love, something you can breathe in when I am no longer here.

MICHELLE
What about Jeremy?

PAUL
I'm doing my best to give him a lifetime of Dad in the time we have left.
And piss him off just enough, so he'll be OK when I go. Nothing left
unsaid. Everything forgiven. Yes... Even Joe. He was my friend.
Something snapped, and he lost it. He was hurting. I can forgive him, but
I know it will take time for everyone else.

MICHELLE
Yes. Not everyone has the luxury of a dead spouse to help them with
their thinking.
(pause)
So, what now?

PAUL
We have dinner, I guess. We wait. We enjoy being together.
(to JEREMY)
Pizza or Chirping Chicken?

JEREMY
(offstage)
My answer is always pizza.

PAUL
(to MICHELLE)
You'll have to order it, my left hand just... um... left.

MICHELLE
This is happening way too fast. Can I hug you?

PAUL
Get it while you can.

MICHELLE runs over and gives him a long hug.

PAUL
I'm still here.

MICHELLE
Jeremy!

JEREMY comes out and joins the embrace. There is a group hug as the...

LIGHTS FADE

END OF SCENE

SCENE 4

A few days later at the apartment. MICHELLE cautiously enters the living room.

MICHELLE
Paul?

PAUL
Still here.

Only PAUL's head is visible. Upon seeing him, MICHELLE screams.

PAUL
I know. I look like the great and powerful Wizard of Oz. Sadly, there is no man behind the curtain.

MICHELLE
Oh, sweetie. I am so sorry.

She runs over and kisses him.

MICHELLE
Your lips are so soft.

PAUL
They are fading. I tried to lick a cup of coffee this morning like a cat, but my tongue went right through. I was, however, able to turn on the coffee maker with my nose, so there is coffee.

MICHELLE
Thanks. But my adrenaline is in overdrive right now. Do you think today is the day?

PAUL

Pretty sure. Last night I was head and shoulders above the rest – ha-ha. But by 5am, the neck went fast. Oh, well. No ties for Father's Day this year.

MICHELLE

This may seem weird, but–

PAUL

No weirder than breakfast with a disembodied head.

MICHELLE

John. He'd like to come by.

PAUL

Yes, of course. I'd love to see him, while my eyes still see.

MICHELLE

He feels terrible about this whole thing. He loves you and– well, he'd like to come say goodbye.

PAUL

By all means. Better get him here quick before my ears dissolve.

MICHELLE

I'd better wake Jeremy.

MICHELLE exits off stage. PAUL practices making funny faces. Rolling his eyes. Like he is exercising to keep them alive. JEREMY enters.

JEREMY

Holy–

PAUL

Yes. I seem to be transitioning rather rapidly.

JEREMY
So, today's the day huh?

PAUL
Pretty sure. Mom's texting John. Hope that's OK. He was and still is the
best friend I ever had. We need some closure. A passing of the torch, so
to speak. I don't want any of you to feel guilty about starting again, as a
family of three. I am here. And no, I won't be able to see you once my
eyes go. I won't be able to touch you, but I am around. Molecules in the
air, then atoms, then I guess… whatever there is that is smaller than an
atom until–

JEREMY
WAIT!

JEREMY runs off stage and returns with a glass bell jar.

JEREMY
Breathe into this, Dad. Just don't drop an eyeball in or anything, cause
they would totally freak me out.

*PAUL smiles. He breathes into the jar several times, whispers words we
cannot hear. JEREMY quickly grabs the jar and screws the lid on tight.*

JEREMY
This is so when the air starts to circulate, or mom opens a window, I'll
still have you with me.

PAUL
That's sweet, son.

JEREMY
Yesterday, Ginny Taylor started talking to me. She's the smartest girl in
the 7th grade. She came right up to me and said, "I'm sorry." I thought
she bumped into me, or took my textbook or something, so I said "About
what?" She says "Your dad. I'm so sorry about your dad. I just lost mine,
so I know how you feel." It hit me that I forgot you were dead.

JEREMY (Cont.)

Now you're going to be dead again, but I am in a different place. I knew what to say. She said that her dad was the one to lift her up when she felt down. I told her he can lift her up from where he is now... I promise. It's true, isn't it? I will be able to feel you. It's like sugar in coffee. You can't see it, but you know it's there.

MICHELLE

John's downstairs.

PAUL

That was quick.

MICHELLE

I actually called him last night. He's been sitting in the coffee shop since 6am. Need anything?

PAUL

I'd love a toasted bagel, but without a stomach or a neck, it might not be a pretty sight.

MICHELLE gives him a quick kiss.

MICHELLE

Can you feel that?

PAUL

Yup. Better than ice cream.

JEREMY winces at the PDA, but says nothing. There is a knock at the door.

JEREMY

I'll get it.

JEREMY opens the door. JOHN is standing there sheepishly with a bag of bagels and cookies.

JEREMY
WOW! You brought bagels. Just in time. At least dad can still smell them.

JEREMY rushes over to PAUL with the bag of bagels.

PAUL
AH!! My last quintessential New York smell. I hope they have bagels wherever I wind up.

JOHN stars incredulously at PAUL, maybe drops the bag of bagels.

JOHN
Oh, my God!!

JEREMY
Dad's always been a head of his time, right?

PAUL
Hey, leave those dad jokes to me.

JOHN
What can I say? What can I do? You were... are, my best friend. I never meant to step on your toes.

PAUL
No chance of that anymore. Look, you two. There was no intent to hurt me. I know that. I am not hurt. I am grateful. Do not wear guilt like handcuffs, like a rope around your necks. It will crush you. Weigh you down.

MICHELLE
I don't think I'll ever stop loving you, Paul.

PAUL

I have been lucky to have had one great love in my life. That's more than most people get. You are lucky enough to have two. Embrace it. It's not whether you are alive or dead, It's what you leave behind that matters. And speaking of that, Jeremy, look under the couch, I left something there.

JEREMY goes and gets a box, full of papers.

JEREMY
What is this?

PAUL

I was writing a book while I still had fingers to type. When I lost those, I tried to dictate, but it was too hard to spellcheck with my nose.

MICHELLE
When did you have the time?

PAUL

When you don't need to sleep, you have nothing but time. I kept thinking, "I'll sleep when I'm dead."

JEREMY
(looking at first page)
"Evanescent, the delicate art of being in the now and then." Good title, dad.

PAUL

I thought it might be helpful. And maybe, John, you can say you "ghost wrote" it. I know you have contacts in the publishing industry. If Michelle wrote it, people might write it off as the wishful thinking of a lunatic grieving wife.

MICHELLE
They might think the same of John. Guilty best friend searching to absolve himself.

JOHN

I don't care what people think. It would be an honor. I love you, man.

PAUL

I'm fading. I can feel it.

MICHELLE

I don't understand. Why you? Why didn't any of the others come back?

PAUL

We don't know they didn't. Maybe, like us, they were afraid to disclose. Maybe the book will help everyone come out of the shadows. A bad thing happened. To all of us. I can't fix that. But I guess the point is that we are all still here. A billion infinitesimal parts of the universe, swirling around. Breathe us in. Quick, come in for a group hug. I know it's like hugging a basketball but...

JOHN, MICHELLE and JEREMY all crowd around PAUL. It is at this time that they can cover him completely with a black blanket so he is unseen.

PAUL

I should have quit while I was a head. Going out with one last dad joke...

JEREMY

We got you, Dad. We've all got you.

They take a moment, then step back. MICHELLE is crying. JOHN puts his arms around her.

JOHN
(to the air)
Don't worry my friend. I've got this.

MICHELLE

I love you... wherever you are.

JEREMY holds up his jar of air.

JEREMY
He's home.

JEREMY puts the jar on the table. He goes to hug his mom as lights fade.

END OF PLAY

ABOUT THE AUTHOR

Bambi Everson is a playwright, actress, and teaching artist. She studied with Geraldine Page and Michael Schulman, and appeared in many Off-Off Broadway productions in her youth. She wrote her first play in 2015, and has since completed over 20 more, including six full-lengths.

Her work tends to incorporate oddball characters and situations, from screwball comedy to dark melodrama, from cannibals in suburban Long Island, to murderous love triangles amongst octogenarians in an assisted living facility. She's been influenced as much by cinema as she has by theater, an inescapable accident of birth, as she's the daughter of noted film historian, William K. Everson.

Her plays have been produced at Manhattan Repertory Theatre, Hudson Guild, Emerging Artists Theatre, The Little Theatre of Alexandria, VA, and college productions in North Carolina and Arkansas. THE THIN MAN IN THE CHERRY ORCHARD was featured at the 2019 New York Fringe Festival. She was the recipient of the 2015 Yip Harburg Foundation award. She teaches playwriting at PPAS in Manhattan, and is a member of The Dramatist's Guild.

Follow her adventures at her website, bambieverson.com.

More plays by Bambi Everson

Visit BambiEverson.com

Made in the USA
Middletown, DE
03 November 2022

14051881R00046